CELLO
BIG BOOK
of Disney SONGS

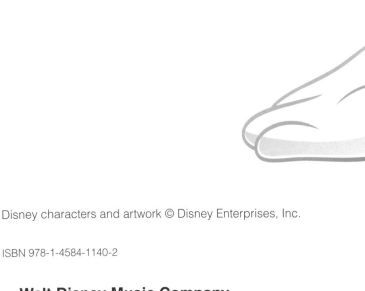

Available for
FLUTE, CLARINET, ALTO SAX, TENOR SAX, TRUMPET,
HORN, TROMBONE, VIOLIN, VIOLA, CELLO

Disney characters and artwork © Disney Enterprises, Inc.

ISBN 978-1-4584-1140-2

Walt Disney Music Company
Wonderland Music Company, Inc.

DISTRIBUTED BY

HAL•LEONARD®
CORPORATION

7777 W. BLUEMOUND RD. P.O. BOX 13819 MILWAUKEE, WI 53213

In Australia Contact:
Hal Leonard Australia Pty. Ltd.
4 Lentara Court
Cheltenham, Victoria, 3192 Australia
Email: ausadmin@halleonard.com.au

Visit Hal Leonard Online at
www.halleonard.com

CONTENTS

ALICE IN WONDERLAND
from Walt Disney's ALICE IN WONDERLAND

CELLO

Words by BOB HILLIARD
Music by SAMMY FAIN

Moderately

THE BALLAD OF DAVY CROCKETT
from Walt Disney's DAVY CROCKETT

Words by TOM BLACKBURN
Music by GEORGE BRUNS

Moderately

BE OUR GUEST

from Walt Disney's BEAUTY AND THE BEAST

Lyrics by HOWARD ASHMAN
Music by ALAN MENKEN

Moderately

THE BARE NECESSITIES

from Walt Disney's THE JUNGLE BOOK

CELLO

Words and Music by
TERRY GILKYSON

BEAUTY AND THE BEAST

from Walt Disney's BEAUTY AND THE BEAST

Cello

Lyrics by HOWARD ASHMAN
Music by ALAN MENKEN

CELLO

BELLA NOTTE
(This Is the Night)
from Walt Disney's LADY AND THE TRAMP

Words and Music by PEGGY LEE
and SONNY BURKE

BIBBIDI-BOBBIDI-BOO
(The Magic Song)
from Walt Disney's CINDERELLA

Words by JERRY LIVINGSTON
Music by MACK DAVID and AL HOFFMAN

CRUELLA DE VIL
from Walt Disney's 101 DALMATIANS

Words and Music by
MEL LEVEN

BREAKING FREE

from the Disney Channel Original Movie HIGH SCHOOL MUSICAL

CELLO

Words and Music by
JAMIE HOUSTON

BEST OF FRIENDS
from Walt Disney's THE FOX AND THE HOUND

CELLO

Words by STAN FIDEL
Music by RICHARD JOHNSTON

CAN YOU FEEL THE LOVE TONIGHT
from Walt Disney Pictures' THE LION KING

CELLO

Music by ELTON JOHN
Lyrics by TIM RICE

Pop Ballad

CANDLE ON THE WATER

from Walt Disney's PETE'S DRAGON

Cello

Words and Music by AL KASHA
and JOEL HIRSCHHORN

CHIM CHIM CHER-EE

from Walt Disney's MARY POPPINS

CELLO

Words and Music by RICHARD M. SHERMAN
and ROBERT B. SHERMAN

Lightly, with gusto

small notes optional

COLORS OF THE WIND
from Walt Disney's POCAHONTAS

CELLO

Music by ALAN MENKEN
Lyrics by STEPHEN SCHWARTZ

A DREAM IS A WISH YOUR HEART MAKES

from Walt Disney's CINDERELLA

Words and Music by MACK DAVID,
AL HOFFMAN and JERRY LIVINGSTON

CIRCLE OF LIFE
from Walt Disney Pictures' THE LION KING

CELLO

Music by ELTON JOHN
Lyrics by TIM RICE

Moderately (with an African beat)

GO THE DISTANCE

from Walt Disney Pictures' HERCULES

CELLO

Music by ALAN MENKEN
Lyrics by DAVID ZIPPEL

FRIEND LIKE ME

from Walt Disney's ALADDIN

CELLO

Lyrics by HOWARD ASHMAN
Music by ALAN MENKEN

GOD HELP THE OUTCASTS

from Walt Disney's THE HUNCHBACK OF NOTRE DAME

CELLO

Music by ALAN MENKEN
Lyrics by STEPHEN SCHWARTZ

HOW D'YE DO AND SHAKE HANDS

from Walt Disney's ALICE IN WONDERLAND

Words by CY COBEN
Music by OLIVER WALLACE

HAKUNA MATATA

from Walt Disney Pictures' THE LION KING

CELLO

Music by ELTON JOHN
Lyrics by TIM RICE

HE'S A TRAMP

from Walt Disney's LADY AND THE TRAMP

Words and Music by PEGGY LEE
and SONNY BURKE

Moderately

I JUST CAN'T WAIT TO BE KING

from Walt Disney Pictures' THE LION KING

CELLO

Music by ELTON JOHN
Lyrics by TIM RICE

I'M LATE
from Walt Disney's ALICE IN WONDERLAND

Words by BOB HILLIARD
Music by SAMMY FAIN

Moderately fast

IF I NEVER KNEW YOU
(Love Theme from POCAHONTAS)
from Walt Disney's POCAHONTAS

CELLO

Music by ALAN MENKEN
Lyrics by STEPHEN SCHWARTZ

IT'S A SMALL WORLD
from Disneyland Resort® and Magic Kingdom® Park

CELLO

Words and Music by RICHARD M. SHERMAN
and ROBERT B. SHERMAN

LAVENDER BLUE
(Dilly Dilly)
from Walt Disney's SO DEAR TO MY HEART

Words by LARRY MOREY
Music by ELIOT DANIEL

LET'S GET TOGETHER
from Walt Disney Pictures' THE PARENT TRAP

Words and Music by RICHARD M. SHERMAN
and ROBERT B. SHERMAN

LET'S GO FLY A KITE
from Walt Disney's MARY POPPINS

CELLO

Words and Music by RICHARD M. SHERMAN
and ROBERT B. SHERMAN

With gusto

MY FUNNY FRIEND AND ME
from Walt Disney Pictures' THE EMPEROR'S NEW GROOVE

Lyrics by STING
Music by STING and DAVID HARTLEY

Moderately

LITTLE APRIL SHOWER
from Walt Disney's BAMBI

CELLO

Words by LARRY MOREY
Music by FRANK CHURCHILL

THE LORD IS GOOD TO ME
from Walt Disney's MELODY TIME
from Walt Disney's JOHNNY APPLESEED

Words and Music by KIM GANNON
and WALTER KENT

MICKEY MOUSE MARCH

from Walt Disney's THE MICKEY MOUSE CLUB

Words and Music by
JIMMIE DODD

KISS THE GIRL

from Walt Disney's THE LITTLE MERMAID

CELLO

Music by ALAN MENKEN
Lyrics by HOWARD ASHMAN

NEVER SMILE AT A CROCODILE

from Walt Disney's PETER PAN

CELLO

Words by JACK LAWRENCE
Music by FRANK CHURCHILL

PART OF YOUR WORLD
from Walt Disney's THE LITTLE MERMAID

CELLO

Music by ALAN MENKEN
Lyrics by HOWARD ASHMAN

ONCE UPON A DREAM
from Walt Disney's SLEEPING BEAUTY

CELLO

Words and Music by SAMMY FAIN
and JACK LAWRENCE
Adapted from a Theme by Tchaikovsky

Flowingly

REFLECTION
from Walt Disney Pictures' MULAN

Music by MATTHEW WILDER
Lyrics by DAVID ZIPPEL

Moderately slow

A PIRATE'S LIFE
from Walt Disney's PETER PAN

CELLO

Words by ED PENNER
Music by OLIVER WALLACE

SCALES AND ARPEGGIOS
from Walt Disney's THE ARISTOCATS

Words and Music by RICHARD M. SHERMAN
and ROBERT B. SHERMAN

THE SECOND STAR TO THE RIGHT

from Walt Disney's PETER PAN

Words by SAMMY CAHN
Music by SAMMY FAIN

SALUDOS AMIGOS

from Walt Disney's SALUDOS AMIGOS
from Walt Disney's THE THREE CABALLEROS

CELLO

Words by NED WASHINGTON
Music by CHARLES WOLCOTT

SO THIS IS LOVE
(The Cinderella Waltz)
from Walt Disney's CINDERELLA

CELLO

Words and Music by MACK DAVID,
AL HOFFMAN and JERRY LIVINGSTON

THE SIAMESE CAT SONG
from Walt Disney's LADY AND THE TRAMP

CELLO

Words and Music by PEGGY LEE
and SONNY BURKE

SOONER OR LATER
from Walt Disney's SONG OF THE SOUTH

Words and Music by RAY GILBERT
and CHARLES WOLCOTT

SOMEDAY
from Walt Disney's THE HUNCHBACK OF NOTRE DAME

CELLO

Music by ALAN MENKEN
Lyrics by STEPHEN SCHWARTZ

SOMEONE'S WAITING FOR YOU
from Walt Disney's THE RESCUERS

CELLO

Words by CAROL CONNORS and AYN ROBBINS
Music by SAMMY FAIN

A SPOONFUL OF SUGAR

from Walt Disney's MARY POPPINS

CELLO

Words and Music by RICHARD M. SHERMAN
and ROBERT B. SHERMAN

THESE ARE THE BEST TIMES

from Walt Disney Productions' SUPERDAD

CELLO

Words and Music by
SHANE TATUM

Tenderly

SWEET SURRENDER

from Walt Disney's THE BEARS AND I

CELLO

Words and Music by
JOHN DENVER

TOYLAND MARCH
from Walt Disney's BABES IN TOYLAND

Adapted from V. HERBERT Melody
Words by MEL LEVEN
Music by GEORGE BRUNS

March tempo

TRASHIN' THE CAMP

from Walt Disney Pictures' TARZAN™

CELLO

Words and Music by
PHIL COLLINS

Moderate Swing

Wooh!

WESTWARD HO, THE WAGONS!

from Walt Disney's WESTWARD HO, THE WAGONS!

Words by TOM BLACKBURN
Music by GEORGE BRUNS

SUPERCALIFRAGILISTICEXPIALIDOCIOUS

from Walt Disney's MARY POPPINS

CELLO

Words and Music by RICHARD M. SHERMAN
and ROBERT B. SHERMAN

Brightly

THE UNBIRTHDAY SONG

from Walt Disney's ALICE IN WONDERLAND

Cello

Words and Music by MACK DAVID,
AL HOFFMAN and JERRY LIVINGSTON

UNDER THE SEA

from Walt Disney's THE LITTLE MERMAID

CELLO

Music by ALAN MENKEN
Lyrics by HOWARD ASHMAN

WE'RE ALL IN THIS TOGETHER

from the Disney Channel Original Movie HIGH SCHOOL MUSICAL

CELLO

Words and Music by MATTHEW GERRARD
and ROBBIE NEVIL

WHEN SHE LOVED ME

from Walt Disney Pictures' TOY STORY 2 - A Pixar Film

CELLO

Music and Lyrics by
RANDY NEWMAN

Tenderly, very freely

WINNIE THE POOH
from Walt Disney's THE MANY ADVENTURES OF WINNIE THE POOH

Words and Music by RICHARD M. SHERMAN
and ROBERT B. SHERMAN

Tenderly

WHERE THE DREAM TAKES YOU

from Walt Disney Pictures' ATLANTIS: THE LOST EMPIRE

CELLO

Lyrics by DIANE WARREN
Music by DIANE WARREN
and JAMES NEWTON HOWARD

Moderately

A WHOLE NEW WORLD

CELLO

from Walt Disney's ALADDIN

Music by ALAN MENKEN
Lyrics by TIM RICE

A WHALE OF A TALE

from Walt Disney's 20,000 LEAGUES UNDER THE SEA

CELLO

Words and Music by NORMAN GIMBEL
and AL HOFFMAN

THE WONDERFUL THING ABOUT TIGGERS

from Walt Disney's THE MANY ADVENTURES OF WINNIE THE POOH

Words and Music by RICHARD M. SHERMAN
and ROBERT B. SHERMAN

YO HO
(A Pirate's Life for Me)
from PIRATES OF THE CARIBBEAN at Disneyland Park and Magic Kingdom Park

Words by XAVIER ATENCIO
Music by GEORGE BRUNS

In a robust manner

WRINGLE WRANGLE
(A Pretty Woman's Love)
from Walt Disney's WESTWARD HO, THE WAGONS!

CELLO

Words and Music by
STAN JONES

WRITTEN IN THE STARS

from Elton John and Tim Rice's AIDA

CELLO

Music by ELTON JOHN
Lyrics by TIM RICE

Slowly

YOU ARE THE MUSIC IN ME

from the Disney Channel Original Movie HIGH SCHOOL MUSICAL 2

CELLO

Words and Music by
JAMIE HOUSTON

Moderately fast Rock

YOU'LL BE IN MY HEART

(Pop Version)

from Walt Disney Pictures' TARZAN™

CELLO

Words and Music by
PHIL COLLINS

YOU CAN FLY! YOU CAN FLY! YOU CAN FLY!

CELLO

from Walt Disney's PETER PAN

Words by SAMMY CAHN
Music by SAMMY FAIN

YOU'VE GOT A FRIEND IN ME

from Walt Disney's TOY STORY

CELLO

Music and Lyrics by
RANDY NEWMAN

ZERO TO HERO
from Walt Disney Pictures' HERCULES

CELLO

Music by ALAN MENKEN
Lyrics by DAVID ZIPPEL

ZIP-A-DEE-DOO-DAH

from Walt Disney's SONG OF THE SOUTH

CELLO

Words by RAY GILBERT
Music by ALLIE WRUBEL